Prayers to Live

Peter Neff

World rights reserved. This book or any portion thereof may not be copied or reproduced in any form or manner whatever, except as provided by law, without the written permission of the publisher, except by a reviewer who may quote brief passages in a review.

The author assumes full responsibility for the accuracy of all facts and quotations as cited in this book. The opinions expressed in this book are the author's personal views and interpretations and do not necessarily reflect those of the publisher.

Copyright © 2013 Aspect Books
ISBN-13: 978-1-4796-0159-2 (Paperback)
ISBN-13: 978-1-4796-0160-8 (ePub)
ISBN-13: 978-1-4796-0161-5 (Kindle / Mobi)
Library of Congress Control Number: 2013909119

Published by

www.ASPECTBooks.com

I dedicate this book of poems
to God, to His inspiration,
to my mom and dad, my brother too,
and God's bride, His church.
—*Peter*

Peter was born in 1980 and has Down syndrome. He took an interest in poetry and began his writing career in middle school. He lives with his parents in Olympia, Washington, goes to work every day, volunteers in his community, and takes an active role in his church. He loves God, his family, his pets, blowing bubbles, listening to worship music, and drawing. His unique art was used to illustrate this book.

Foreword

Peter has authored an astounding number of poems. This book is comprised of the smallest excerpt of the smallest portion of his collection. The writing flows from Peter. For every situation there is a commentary, for every occasion a memento, for every disappointment a lament, and in every moment there is praise for God. Whenever he meets someone new, wherever he is, he invariably sets to composing for them, if time allows. His poems have blessed many with their kind and beautiful words. This is Peter's gift to us.

It seems right that such a prolific and gifted poet should be known for his work. It seems right that his creations should be available for other to enjoy and treasure. The moment has finally come for Peter's long-time dream and goal to be realized. I pray that God will be honored, and that Peter's accomplishments will be recognized through the production and distribution of this collection. His readers are sure to be blessed as they get to know God through his eyes in this, the first of many more to come, book of Peter's poems.

—Josh

Table of Contents

A Prayer to Live This New Year 9

My World 10

You and I: Each Other's Shelter 11

Mother 13

Our Immortal God Has a Human Heart 14

Perfection Is 15

The Cost of Grace 16

In Your Tears (and Through Them All) 17

Matter Over Mind 19

My Dove's Magic Kiss and My
   Magic Touch 21

Beauty Fairest Sings 22

I am So Very Sure and I am So Very Certain 23

Could it Be? 24

May We Be the Apple of Your Eye 25

Stephen 26

Lovable Peaceableness 29

Come and See 30

What a Friend 31

Go to Jesus and Come Back to Me 33

Mary Magdalene	34
Forgiven and Accused	35
God Promised	36
Ink	37
How to Teach an Animal Submission and Obedience	39
The Piano	40
Marriage Isn't Out of Date	42
There's Nothing Better Than a Subdued Heart	43
You My Family Living With Me	44
A Spiritual Song Is	45
Beloved Brother	47
Getting Real With Jesus	48
Live the Wonder	49
A Letter From A Good, Unfallen, and Entertained Angel	51
Tell Me the Story of Jesus	52
Standing Up For Jesus	53
The Darkness is Helpless (Hallelujah!)	55
Sanctuary for the Moment	57
Melody Heavenly	58
Let Us Pray	59

A Prayer to Live This New Year
1/1/2005

Beautiful, heavenly Father
Of fairness and grace.

How great Thou art,
How small I be.

You alone are worthy,
I'm undeserving.

How right are Your chosen
To adore You,
For You are wonderful.

I confess
I have not "known" You
As I ought.

I thank You for
Your Son; the blessing
Above all blessings
And everything good.

And I pray
For help, this new year,
To live this prayer
And I thank You
For it.

In Jesus' name,
Amen.

My World
7/16/1998

In my world
Are my families of the
Spirit.

In my world
Are homes of the
New life
In the Spirit.

In my world
All nature is
Celestial,
Every season
Is forever present
In sight.

In my world
Gardens are free
Of the curse.
Gardens and their
Holders forever flourish.

In my world
All animals, every insect
And teems of the water
Are healed from sin's sting.

In my world
Health and life
Are full and
Ever-filling.

In my world
Futility has been
Cast out
And relationships
Show equality,
Unity, and brotherly
Love.

In my world
The fruits
Of the Spirit
Flood the new life.

In my world
There is bright
And outstanding perfect
Beauty.

There is grace,
There is peace,
There is comfort and
Relaxation.
Even Heaven's music
Fills my world.

In my world
Every person is our neighbor,
Family and friend,
Even brother and sister!

In my world
Are families of the
Spirit.

My world is
Heaven.

You and I: Each Other's Shelter
10/2/2004

Let us be
Each other's shelter;
Gentle and tender,
Fair and gracious.

You and I
Refreshing each other;
We will enjoy
Being each other's
Selfless blessing.

You and I
Restoring one another;
We will delight in our
Blessed reunion.

You and I;
May we be
To each other
A shelter peaceable.

Mother
5/10/1998

Such delicate rose
A celestial rose;
The angel of
Your love and beauty
Holds it in her
Right hand.

Though there
May be thorns
Brambles, briars
And weeds,
Your spirit overlooks
Them.

Lift up your eyes.
Do not let life
Sift you as wheat,
Do not let it
Strain your spirit
Out.

Your light shines
Through
The rose
Which you are.
The angel
Which your spirit is
Shines the
Light of being
The kind of mother
Whose life the thorns
Will never "know", except me, your son.

Our Immortal God Has a Human Heart
8/12/1999

God has a Son
And His name is Jesus.

God is love,
He sent His son
To us to show us
God through Him.

God so loved us;
Jesus showed us
His care for our need
Of salvation.

God gave us His love,
And we tried His Son in
　judgment.

All that while
God's Son shone His light
In our darkness
And we nailed Him
To the cross because of it.

He was sad and hurt,
He was angry and serious
Only for the right reasons.
He delighted in faith,
Goodness and kindness.
He also made friends
Out of uncommon folk.

God's Son
Was mistreated
In many ways.

To insult
He returned kindness
And such.

He did not come
To condemn,
He came to show
His Father's love
And taught us
All that He is.
Is that really a crime?
Jesus is God's human heart!

Perfection Is
2/22/1999

Perfection is
Always doing what is
Right and good;
That is perfection and righteousness.

Perfection is
Being free from sin;
No longer constrained to do
What is wrong!

Perfection is
Something wonderful
When the soul is cleansed
Through and through.

Perfection is
A beautiful thing.
It is lovely and pure as white,
It makes one innocent.

Only by will, choice and decision
We do things and say things.

God is the only perfect one.
He is our Creator, therefore
He wants us to be perfect.

Perfection is freedom, wonderful, beautiful,
And being someone who always does what is right and good.

The Cost of Grace
3/31/2006

Thank God
His mercies
Are forever free!

Even though
I'm undeserving
He understands why
I pity myself.

And yet, that shouldn't
Be an excuse for me to
Justify it!

The cross of suffering, persecution,
Trial, cruelty, and fatal exposure
To the lengthening of dying
I believe is the cost,

Even though
I prefer
The spiritual
Side of things.

In Your Tears (and Through Them All)
10/22/2011

No tongue can still,
Nor cause to stop
The work of the angel
In the world.

Our Father who is
In heaven alone decides
What shall be His mission,
And message;

So shall we ever be wading in the shore water
Of earth's silver springs,
And heaven's dew angel.

Our Father who is in heaven
Lists your tears
On a scroll,
And collects them
In His heaven-made bottle.

In your tears
He answers the prayers
Of the Spirit that is
In your spirit, and through
Them all you see His
Hand of True love.

Matter Over Mind
4/23/2002

The ink well is
Strangely glowing
And the feather pen
Is also, as well as
Shifting.

The paperweight
Blotter and many other
Writing objects
Move about the room.

The book shelves are filling themselves
With the glowing, shifting, blank books that
Fill themselves with strangely colored pages
And their pages manipulate the pen.

The pen stabs its user, the poisoning strangely fades away.
The writer's flesh turns into ink
And his aura into glow.
His sense of humanism slips away into the oblivion
And the matter
Around him turns his mind
Into the mind of his story.

My Dove's Magic Kiss and My Magic Touch
7/16/1998

An early morning's
Fresh dew and iridescent
Mist surrounds
Me and my dove.

Moons beams
And silvery white
Array glimmers
Upon us.

The lightest rain
Pitter patters softly
At a gracefully dancing
Pace continuously
Around us.

Though dark is the early
    morning
My dove is a light
Surrounding me in
Her radiance.

I give my dove
My magic touch.

Her eyes shimmer
And shine,
Her white dress
Banded of rainbows
Glimmers, her long glowing

Blonde hair and
Her skin twinkles
The light of mine.
Her face and
Form beam and
Gleam.

An early morning's
Fresh dew and iridescent
Mist surrounds me and my
    dove.

The stars
Shimmer like gems
Sewn onto black lace.

My dove
Gives me her
Magic kiss.

My eyes glint
And gleam
My own suit
Glows sending the
Rain away from me.

My countenance and
Being are sparkling
With my dove's
Love's light, her love light
Is me and I am full
Of my light's sparkles.

Beauty Fairest Sings
5/14/2001

Of Jesus' glorious
Majesty and heart
Of hearts;
Of His judgment, justly pronounced, fulfilling
of His justice, as just
As compassion is fair
And of His awesome, almighty
Divinity that imparts
Unto us a life that does it
Justice;
Beauty fairest sings.

Of God as the Creator
Of His pleasure and
Of hearts to be sealed
Upon His almighty right arm,
Of strength, steadfastly
Faithful and true;
Of His love that keeps
His own chosen people
Faithful and true unto Him;
Of His grace that keeps
His own cherished children
Humble and tender
Unto his touch, enriching,
And of his likeness that blesses us.

With the heart of Jesus;
Beauty fairest sings.

I am So Very Sure and I am So Very Certain

3/5/1999

"If we confess our sins
He is faithful and just
And will forgive us our sins
And purify us from
All unrighteousness."

I know that as I
Ask for forgiveness,
Whatever I ask to be forgiven,
The very minute I confess,
My guilt and sin are taken away and
Forgotten.

I believe that Jesus
Is my personal Savior;
He died for me
Just to save me;
I accept the gift of salvation.

I am thankful without measure
For I believe I have received
Forgiveness; So then I am at peace
And am relieved of the presence
Of my accusers!

I am joyous without end
For I thank my Savior
For being so merciful and gracious
When all of my sins
Have been put aside, making me
Feel His presence.
Within Jesus;
If I am in Him and He in me,
He will keep me from sinning, or if
God helped me to overcome
Lawlessness all of the way
His Spirit would protect and
Lead me safely.

I believe this is so;
Jesus is my hope,
In Him I take courage,
Jesus is my strength,
In Him I am determined,
Jesus is with me always,
In Him I am bold and fearless,
In Him I am strong.

Jesus is my encouragement and
My Healer; He is my All,
The Lord of my heart and a
Wonderful heavenly Brother
And True Friend.

I believe this to be so too;
All this is certainty!
The Only Son of God;
The Holy Lamb of God
Is my Savior
And He gives me salvation
And forgiveness of sins,
Therefore, I am so very sure, so very certain.

Could it Be?
10/2/2004

Could it be
That we have
Played ring around
The rosy thorn bush
For too long?

Could it be
That we are
Having too much fun
With our pockets
Bulging full of posies?

Could it be
That we were
The ones who fell into
The wooing of the rosies?

And could it be possible
To shake off the spell
Before it's too late
And we dizzy each other
Into the thorn bush?

May We Be the Apple of Your Eye
10/23/2007

Heavenly Abba Father,

Your name is wonderful,
And precious above all.

We have not known You
As we ought, and are
Very weak, and needy,
And we are sheep.

We give You thanks
For Your kindness;
Because it leads to
True repentance, and
Is better than
This life!

And so we pray—
May we be the apple
Of Your eye, and a people
After Your own heart
Even though
We are sheep.

In Jesus' name,
Amen, and Amen.

Stephen
12/17/1999

One of seven
Chosen men;
A man full of faith
And of the Holy Spirit.

The seven men
Were presented
Unto God's chosen
Apostles who
Prayed and laid
Their hands on them.

One of seven
Chosen men;
A man full of God's
Grace and Power
Who did great wonders
And miraculous signs.

Opposition arose against him,
Certain Jews and
Certain member of a
Certain church
Picked verbal fights with him.
Accusations rose against him
  on every side,
Stirring up people, elders and
Teachers in law against him,
Seizing and manipulation of
  him.
False witness was against him,
And the Sanhedrin
Saw that Stephen's face was
  like
The face of an angel's.

The high priest
Questioned him about
His charges
And Stephen gave
His Holy Spirit inspired
Speech.

All who were
Sitting in the Sanhedrin,
When they heard it, they
Became furious and
They gnashed their teeth
At him.

Full of the Holy Spirit, Stephen
  looked up
To Heaven and
Saw God's glory
And at His right hand
He saw Jesus standing.

"Look,
I see Heaven open
And the Son of Man
Standing at the
Right hand of God,"
He said.

Those in the
Sanhedrin
Covered their ears
And yelled
At the top of their voices,
Rushing at him
Dragging him
Out of the city
And began to stone him.

At the feet
Of a young man
Named Saul
Who persecuted those
Of Stephen's sort,
Clothes were laid.

While the Sanhedrin
Stoned Stephen,
Stephen prayed for
Their forgiveness
After commending
His Spirit back to God.

Lovable Peaceableness
10/4/2004

Lovable peaceableness;
It is a blessing and a joy,
And a precious treasure.

Lovable peaceableness;
Let it be
Both your cloak
And tunic.

Lovable peaceableness;
If you would
Love him,
He will promote you.

Lovable peaceableness;
If you would
Live for him, and only him always,
He will live his life
Through you
24/7.

Come and See
9/17/2004

Come
And see the gentle
Man of men
And humanity.

Come
And see Him
In your place
Pleading for you.

Come
And see Him
As your only example
To follow.

Come
And see Him
Who is your
Only peace, only way.

Come
And see our gentleman-
Brother, who,
By His stripes, gives everyone true peace.

What a Friend
10/18/2007

Jesus is the kind
Of friend who sees
Us through, and remains
Faithful, and true.

He is honest, and kind;
Fair, and gentle-
What a friend Jesus is.

Jesus is the kind of friend
Who encourages moral character,
And helps us to attain it.

He is divine, and humble;
Righteous, and merciful-
What a friend Jesus is.

His glory is goodness,
And His holiness is honest grace.

Jesus is bold enough
To be forgiving,
And tender hearted enough
To be patient, and zealous for
The beauty of the Lord's name
And His perfect integrity.
What a friend Jesus is.

And He looks for fellowship.

Go to Jesus and Come Back to Me
9/16/2004

Go to Jesus
The Prince of
True peace;
Go to Him
Who is the King
Of true glory
And come back
To me.

Go to Jesus
Just as you are;
Go to Him
Who is and will
Always be
Your one and only
Faithful and true brother
And come back
To me.

Remain kept in His heart
That I may rejoice in
The joy of yours
In Him.

Mary Magdalene
3/27/2004

O what fragrant love
Is yours!

The poured out
Tears of your heart mingle with
The flowing perfume
And your constant kisses
Have prepared
Jesus for His
Burial.

The Lamb of God,
Prince of Peace,
And Lord of Lords
Commends you graciously;
"Wheresoever this Gospel is preached
What Mary Magdalene
Has done for the son of man
Will be remembered."

Dear Mary;
Healed and fulfilled by Jesus,
Someday I will find you
Sitting at His feet again
In the new heaven and earth.

Forgiven and Accused
3/18/1999

I sinned as many sins
As the number
Of the stars and sand.
Half of all of them
Were on accident,
The other half of them all
Were on purpose because of
   sin.

I have hurt others;
Those who I have
Never hated, never even
Wanted to hurt them,
But sin seduced and enticed
   me
As subtly as the serpent
Unclothed Eve of her
   sinlessness!

I wasn't meant to be
A sinner, but because
The serpent manipulated Eve,
And Eve offered Adam
The forbidden fruit of
   knowledge
Of Good and Evil,
And Adam, because of his
   concern
For Eve, I had to be born
With the nature to wander
From my Creator.

Because of Lucifer's
Pride and arrogance and
Because of the serpent's
Cunning, I had to be
Constrained by impulse to
Do Satan's will.
Just doing
What is wrong
Pleases Satan
And hurts God so!

If compulsion to do wrong
Catches me off guard
Or when compulsion to do
   wrong
Takes me by surprise,
A sevenfold demon
May be trying to bind me
To its seven cords
If I do not do anything
About it, since I might not
   notice it.

I know I still sin
But I ask for forgiveness,
I accept it,
I believe I have received it
And I thank my personal
   Savior
So very much!

"If we confess
Our sins He is faithful and
Just to forgive us our sins
And to cleanse us from
All unrighteousness"

My Savior
Can be yours; He is merciful
And gracious to all!

God Promised

Date unknown

"In your language
I will speak
To you,"
God promised
Through the sign
On the cross.

"I will let you choose,"
God promised
Through the two crosses
Beside Jesus
To the left and right.

In the pathway
Up the hill of Jesus' passion
God promised,
"I will never, never
Leave you alone."

In the seamless garment
Of Jesus, God promised,
"I will give you my robe."

Through the
Broken, tortured flesh
Of Jesus
God promised,
"Into my presence
I invite you."

In the gall and
Vinegar filled sponge
Offered unto Jesus' thirst
God promised,
"I understand your pain."

In the gushing torrent of blood
    and water
From Jesus' side
That was pierced,
God promised,
"I have redeemed you
And will always keep you."

God Promised,
"I will love you forever,"
In the cross of Jesus.
In the burial clothing
Of Jesus
God promises,
"I am able, more than able, to
Turn all your tragedies
Into perfect and true
Triumphs."

In the empty tomb
And over death,
The grave, sin,
And the evil one
God has promised,
"I have won
The victory."
Now here there be
A personal question
Put unto you,

What will you
Leave behind
To put all your trust
In God, His promises
And His only answer to you;
Jesus Christ who kept
His only one Heavenly Father's promises?

Ink
9/3/2003

Swish, swish, and swish
Floating, floating
And floating

Flit, flit, and flit,
Flying, flying and
Flying

Scribbling, scribbling
And scribbling

Darting, darting
And darting

Stapple,
Blooop,
 Glurpp,
  Shoop,
   Flowing, flowing
And flowing

Splurting, splurting
And splurting

Glopp, glopp
And glopp

Puddle, puddle
And puddle
Splash, splash
And splash

Wipe, blur,
Wipe, blur and wipe

How to Teach an Animal Submission and Obedience Without Terrorizing It
2/15/2004

Show your animal
Love and respect;
Submit to its demonstrative
Adoration and affection
Of you, and be
Obedient to its education
Of you.

Though your animal
Is just an animal,
Emotionally it is
Just as human as you are, so
Why not humble yourself
And give it honor?

Why not also
Be trained by your animal
To become its own
Faithful and true friend?

Because,
In a sense,
Animals are
Human, and
Humans are
Animals.

The Piano (Let the Rolling Tide of Music Loosen Your Bonds)
7/1/1998

Play whatever
You are feeling
Let your mind go free
Let your eyes wander
From this world
Set aside premade
Emotions which take
Your own expression away.

Make ready
Your fingers for flowing;
Let your hands
Become alive.
Let the rolling
Tide of music
Loosen your bonds
Lose yourself in its
Wave, clash within its
Peace and sweetness.

Let the rolling
Tide of music
Loosen your bonds.

Go with the flow
Even take the freewheeling
And tumbling surf.

Ride upon the
Rising and falling
Fountainous waves
Float among the ripples.

Let the rolling
Tide of music
Loosen your bonds.
Let the tide
Make pools
Let the pools
Stream.

Twirl with the
Water flurries.

Toss and turn
In the wake.

Let the rolling
Tide of music
Loosen your bonds.

Lose yourself
In its wave
Let it take you away
Join in with the
Gushing white and clear.

Flow along with the current
Even ride the rapids
And roll with the incoming
Twirling and spinning beams
Of water.

Most of all
Keep losing yourself
Keep your mind free
Keep flowing
And keep your eyes
Away from this world
Only for a while longer.

Marriage Isn't Out of Date
6/29/2004

Courtship's
Never out of date;
Those kindnesses
Sweetly surprising,
Those tenders
Of submission; beautiful.

Intimacy's
Never out of date;
Those kisses and hugs,
Those smiles and tears,
Those laughs and cries,
Those ups and downs,
Those ins and outs,
Those words within actions,
Those deeds agreeable with words.

Marriage's living
Is never out of date;
Wedlock's joys and sorrows,
Wedlock's blessings and trials,
Wedlock's fragrance and sufferings.

There's Nothing Better Than a Subdued Heart
6/9/2004

The beauty of grace
Softens the hard heart.

The blessing of grace
Waters the dry heart.

The refreshment of grace
Renews the poor heart.

The healing of grace
Completely restores the plagued heart.

The reconciliation of grace
Subdues and forgives the graceless heart.

And there's nothing better
Than a gentle, kind heart,
A satisfied, content heart,
A renewed and enriched heart,
A restored, healed, and cured heart,
And a reconciled, subdued and forgiven heart.

You My Family Living With Me
8/26/2012

I will never be able to
Have a girlfriend,
I will never be able to
Get married,
And I'm already
Incapable of prospering
Like my brother;
Or you; Mom and Dad.

But I have nothing
To complain about;
For I am loved.

Tho' I can
Frustrate you,
You still love me.

Sometimes I wonder
If I have been an inconvenience.
And I feel
Like asking you,
"Are you proud
Of who I am,
Or not?"

I know I'm different,
And that my reason
Is about to fall
Off its rocker;
For it has a flickering
Balance and strength
As it sits on the edge

Of its rocker.
You assure me
That I do have
Your appreciation,
And I do believe you.
Still, on the outside
I'm happy, hoping that I'm loving,
    and really am having fun;
But on the inside
I'm dreaming of moral
    dependence
And wishing for mental
    independence.

And as I drive all of you
Up the wall,
And down the other; as with a pen,
By my awkward
Attempts at claiming
Poetic license in all my
Conversation of Soul
And tongue, I hope
I haven't lost touch
With more than
Reality, reason, and sense,
Or even all of you;
My family, and Him
Who still loves me
Greater than all others.

You and me;
We are meant to come
Back to the place
Where we have nothing
To complain about;
And just be content
With one another,
Building each other up,
And just dwell in the peaceful
   bubbles of
Our living and loving Father of
   Lights.

A Spiritual Song Is
5/8/2004

An Inspiring
Sweet,
Pleasant,
Iridescent,
Refreshing,
Irresistible,
Trusting,
Untiring,
Adoring, and
Living
Song
Of
Noble
Grace

Beloved Brother
5/14/2001

My own brother,
Jesus be in you,
With you,
All about and around you.
And by your side;
His hand in yours though
He is also above you
And shown through you.

Beloved brother,
Jesus' glory and beauty
Be perfected and enriched
In and through you!

Wonderful brother,
You be one of the dearest
Most beautiful angels
From unto glory, fairest!

Beautiful, dearest brother,
You are my own brother
Beloved and wonderful;
Jesus envelopes you
In the fold
Of His likeness in which
A brother is made
In His likeness.

Getting Real With Jesus
8/19/2009

Let us pour out
Our hearts unto Jesus;
How we feel about Him
And the feelings
And the thoughts
We have of Him
And for Him
Desperately and frankly
With sincerest tones
Of adoration, cherishing,
And intimacy; as long as we
Have breath.

Holding it in isn't love,
Neither is it love
To abuse; to misuse
This precious blessing
Before Him.

He sees all, forgives confessed sins,
He hears all, is generous towards all,
And He is holy truth
In all His healing
And cleansing.

And that's just
All the more reason
To get real with Him
And desperately, frankly, cling to Him.

Live the Wonder
9/5/2007

The divine nature of Jesus
Is better lived
By those who choose
To hide in Jesus,
And alienated from all sin.

The wonderful name of Jesus
Is the wonder
To be lived eternally;
And so, let us surrender
To His beauty of character,
And His grace
That we may live
In mercy, and truth.

And let us live, in Christ alone,
The wonder of grace,
And of perfect righteousness,
So that we may be
Clear enough for
Everyone to see
Only Jesus in us.

So I pray that
The beautiful spirit of Jesus
Will adorn, and grace us,
And empty us of all
That is contrary to truth,
And righteousness; grace,
And spiritual love.

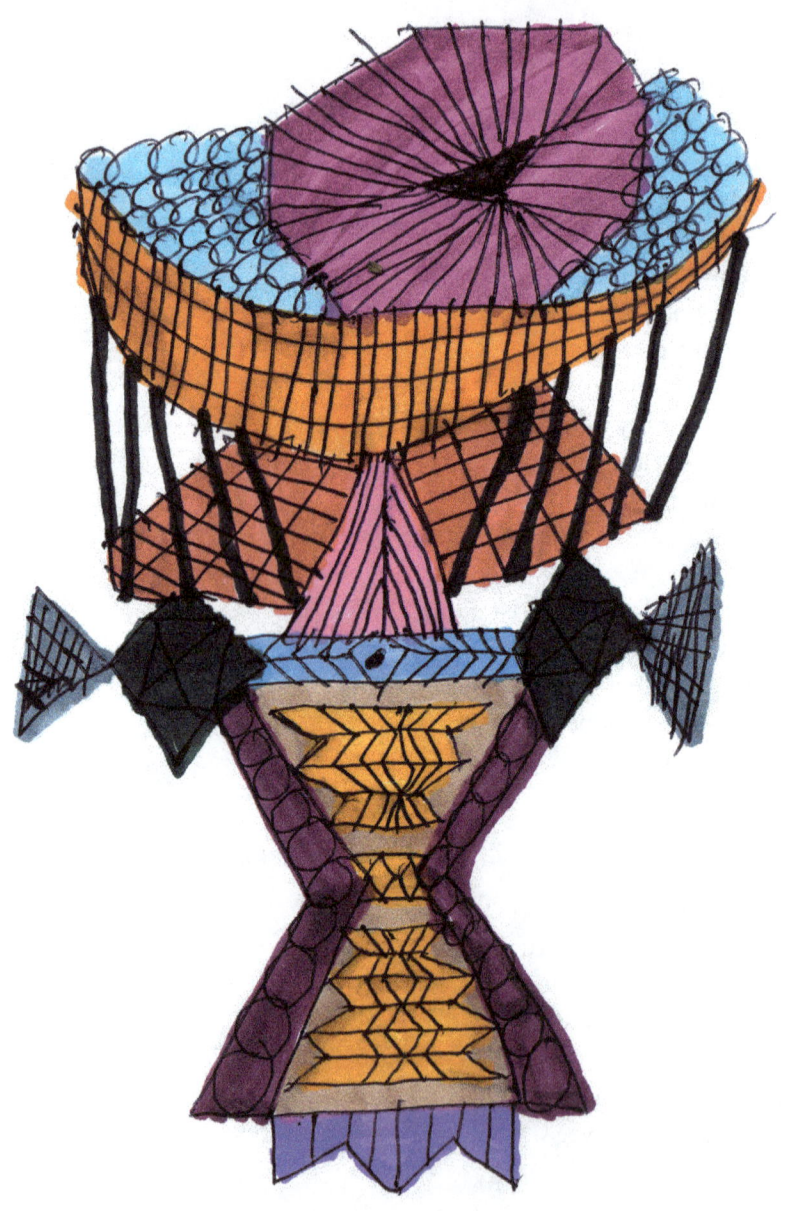

A Letter From A Good, Unfallen, and Entertained Angel
8/23/2009

Beloved precious soul,

I praise the LORD for the blessedness of Jesus that you are putting on.

Tho' you are in the process of coming out of the woods of the world, because of Him alone, I praise the LORD for blessing the earth He has created with the precious gift of you.

And as you are still coming out of the woods of the world, the gift that is above all gifts, Jesus Christ who is LORD and everything unto us, I choose to encourage you to continue to cling to Him and continue to "entertain" His messengers of whom I'm the least.

All thanks and all sorts of glory be unto God the Father, God the Son, and God the Holy Spirit for all the good works They have started, and will finish in you; O faithful and true follower of my LORD, who is our precious everything.

Thanks be unto Jesus for refreshing me through you; and those who live with you in Him.

-Your Friend;
The least of all the Lord's messengers, a servant of His church, a simple friend of His, and a brother of yours in Jesus

Tell Me the Story of Jesus
9/7/2009

Tell me of Jesus;
Teach me His way
With what you know
And believe.

Tell me again His news,
And about His sorrows,
About His pains,
And His sufferings;
Lest I forget
And forget how to put on
His Spirit's fruit,
And His mind.

Sing it over again to me
Those wonderful words
Of the hymn
"Tell Me the Story of Jesus,"
Lest I put a foot
In my mouth
When I speak of
His goodness, and pure heart
With an imperfect voice
And a dark minor key.

Tho' I love to display as I wish
The wonders of
His grace, and the authority
Of His awesome wisdom,
Truth, and power that are
Laced with a love
That is pure, and holy Which
cannot dwell
With impurity, or unholiness
Except with the
Lowly, despised,
Frail and weak.

I should not
Trust myself
With that right;
With that precious work,

For I might slip
On a banana peel of
Someone's motive
Which stands behind
The upheld word
Of divine scripture
If I entrust my guard to the pastor
Over a
"Thus saith an opinion
Of a member
Of Christ's body;
The Church."

So, please tell me the story
Of Jesus that I may still
Love to tell of Jesus' love.

Standing Up For Jesus
9/6/2009

When you are
Truly converted,
Stand up for Jesus.

When you are baptized,
Rise up to bear
"The cross" and for Jesus' sake.

As you learn of Him
To live for the Lord,
Stand up for them.

As you grow in Jesus,
And in His grace,
Stand up for His majestic name.

And when you are
Persecuted for
His righteousness sake,
Still stand up in His spirit
Of grace and faithfulness
For the Lord.

When you choose to all the way
Walk in His footsteps,
By His grace alone,
Stand as you walk in them
Tho' all bloody hell breaks out
All over the world.
For the sake of Jesus.

The Darkness is Helpless (Hallelujah!)
9/25/2007

He who is in you
Is greater than he
Who is in the world;

He who is in you
Exposes the deeds
Of darkness, and casts
Them down.

Overcome evil
With whatsoever is honestly good; and
Put off the deeds
Of darkness, in the Lord,
And you will, by Jesus alone,
Render the darkness helpless.

Praise the Lord
Who helps you to put out
The fiery darts of the devil;
Praise the Lord
Who strengthens you
To move out of the way
The stumbling stones;
Praise the Lord
Who lifts up your head
Against the shadows
Of every temporary night.

Sanctuary for the Moment
8/20/2010

This is the moment
For being overshadowed
By the Most High
And the Dove of His;

For basking in the glow
Of Their true love,
And tender loving care divine;

And feeling and experiencing
The sanctuary that they are.

The precious bundle
Of joy and adventure
Resting peacefully
Within you is filled
With delight in Their designing
The life given, and energy
For the days of life here.

You too are thus loved,
And precious,
And blessed.
For you are a beloved
Daughter of the King of Kings,
And He delights in loving you.

And He with Our Lord Jesus
And all His good angels are
　the sanctuary

For all the moments
That surround you
And your bundle of joy.
The King who loves
All His children,
Of Whom I have written,
Is love, life,
And light;

And is only
A prayer away.

He is our
Heavenly Abba Father
Above all, and all situations.

Divine mercy, and grace,
And true love are
The foundation of His throne;

He never leaves, nor forsakes,
His precious children.

This King of divine love
Forgives, is kind,
And is patient, loyal, and true.

All for loving His own
He risks His reputation;
He would rather be
　misunderstood
Than to push away those
Whom He truly loves.

He is lovingly the Most High,
And it is His good Spirit
That hovers gently
Over you and your own.

Melody Heavenly
9/13/2007

There is a melody
Which sings
Of a joy that springs
Like meadow flowers
In the midst of storms.

There is heavenly music
Which permeates,
Like lovely incense,
Every life in some way.

There is a melody
Which satisfies the empty;
The "poor in spirit,"
And sounds of darkest
Minor key within
The hearts of those
Who hate the God of love,
Life, and light.

There is heavenly music
Which is a blessing
To the receptive of the Lord;
And a curse too sour
To stomach for those who love
To use the power of death.

There is a melody
Which sings of a joy
That springs like meadow flowers
Midst the storms.

Let Us Pray
10/31/2007

Let us pray
For those who are
Told not to pray
In Jesus' name.
Let us pray
For those who are
Told to preach any kind of Jesus,
Except the real Jesus.
Let us pray
For the victims of
Divisive people.
Let us pray
For the needy, and poor
Hungry, and thirsty ones.
Let us pray
For our enemies,
And that we may benefit
From our troubles.
Let us pray
For our families, and friends,
And that we may escape
The spotlight of self-exaltation.
Let us pray
For the misused, and abused.
Let us pray
For those who will come
To the cross for the first time,
And let us pray, last of all,
For our relationship with Jesus.

Special thanks to my friends for their efforts in helping me organize these poems (they know who they are).
And to our wonderful parents.
And to our Lord God above all.

We invite you to view the complete
selection of titles we publish at:

www.AspectBooks.com

Scan with your mobile
device to go directly
to our website.

Please write or email us your praises, reactions, or
thoughts about this or any other book we publish at:

P.O. Box 954
Ringgold, GA 30736

info@AspectBooks.com

Aspect Books titles may be purchased in bulk for
educational, business, fund-raising, or sales promotional use.
For information, please e-mail:

BulkSales@AspectBooks.com

Finally, if you are interested in seeing
your own book in print, please contact us at:

publishing@AspectBooks.com

We would be happy to review your manuscript for free.

www.ingramcontent.com/pod-product-compliance
Lightning Source LLC
Chambersburg PA
CBHW070559160426
43199CB00014B/2552